EMPOWERMENT

A Key Component
of
Christian Community Development

By

Mary Nelson, PhD

EMPOWERMENT
A Key Component of Christian Community Development

iUniverse books may be ordered through booksellers or by contacting:

iUniverse
1663 Liberty Drive
Bloomington, IN 47403
www.iuniverse.com
1-800-Authors (1-800-288-4677)

ISBN: 978-1-4401-8532-8 (pbk)
ISBN: 978-1-4401-8533-5 (ebk)

Library of Congress Control Number: 2009911122

Printed in the United States of America

iUniverse rev. date: 1/13/2010

contents

IV

Preface

The author is deeply indebted to the wisdom and experience of many people who contributed concepts and stories to this curriculum, especially the CCDA Empowerment committee, including: Kit Danley, Bob Lupton, Rudy Carrasco, Juanita Irizarry, Michael Mata; and the CCDA Institute workshop materials from Bob Lupton's workshop on Empowerment. We also want to acknowledge the hard work of CCDA staff, Dave Clark, Pam Toussaint, Matt Hiltibran and Salvador Jimenez in the completion of this project.

Notes

This Empowerment book and a companion DVD have been developed by the Christian Community Development Association (CCDA) as a Toolkit to be used by individuals and ministries with a desire to restore under-resourced communities utilizing the Biblical philosophy of Christian Community Development (CCD). It can be used as a participant's workbook for those attending a CCDA Institute class, a leader's guide for those who wish to teach this material in their ministry setting, and as a resource that CCD practitioners, or those interested in becoming practitioners, can use on their own.

Bible citations are from the New Revised Standard Version, except where noted otherwise.

Forward

Twenty years ago, I moved my family from sunny California to Chicago to establish a ministry in the Mexican community of La Villita using the philosophy of Christian Community Development (CCD) as my guide. When I first heard Dr. John Perkins articulate the mission and vision of CCD, I knew it was an approach that I could embrace as a Christian wanting to make an impact in the lives of my Latino neighbors and in the barrio. Since 1989, I have worked as a CCD practitioner, a CCDA board member and as a staff person of this great association.

In 2006, I took on the challenge of establishing the CCDA Institute to provide our members, and others interested in community transformation with an opportunity to investigate the ministry philosophy of Christian Community Development (CCD).

CCD is a Biblical approach to working in under-resourced communities, which has been developed and championed by Dr. John Perkins and other key CCDA leaders over the last 40 years.

The three R's have been the foundation of our movement.

Relocation
Reconciliation
Redistribution

In the last fifteen years, five other Key Components have been identified as central to the CCD philosophy that we believe is the most effective approach to changing the lives of the poor and transforming under-resourced neighborhoods.

Church-Based
Listening to the Community
Wholistic
Leadership Development
Empowerment

Thanks to the generosity of Philip and Marsha Dowd, CCDA is embarking on creating this new series of 'CCD Toolkits' which includes a book and a companion DVD. These Toolkits will help teach the CCD approach to Christian leaders committed to neighborhood-based ministry.

In the following pages, Dr. Mary Nelson will help us unpack the EMPOWERMENT component. Mary has worked diligently creating opportunities to empower her neighbors and her Westside Chicago community for thirty years. The amazing results include creating new affordable housing, new jobs, dynamic youth and senior programs, and being a spiritual witness. And Mary has accomplished all of this through the leadership of her neighbors—neighbors empowered to lead!

Today, as the CEO of CCDA, my prayer is that Christ followers all over our nation will be equipped to live out our Biblical mandate to passionately love people and communities on the margins of our society. The following Chinese proverb, often quoted by Dr. John Perkins, captures the heart of CCD and particularly, EMPOWERMENT:

> Go to the people,
> Live among them,
> Learn from them,
> Love them,
> Start with what they know,
> Build on what they have:
> But of the best leaders,
> When their task is done,
> The people will remark
> "We have done it ourselves."

For more information about the CCDA Institute, contact us at info@ccda.org.

Noel Castellanos
CEO, CCDA

section **one:** BASIC QUESTIONS ABOUT CCD AND EMPOWERMENT

The eight components of Christian Community Development (CCD) employ a wholistic approach to working with people and under-resourced communities. This approach is a new paradigm, a new way of looking and acting as God's people to transform under-resourced communities. It is sharing God's vision of "wholistically restored communities with Christians engaged in the process of transformation." It is important to note that the focus for CCD is **under-resourced** urban, suburban and rural communities, even though most of the components can also apply elsewhere.

There is overlap between each component, and true CCD needs to incorporate all eight components to be most effective. All eight of the key components of CCD listed below, when lived and applied as a whole, have the power to transform people and communities—picking and choosing one or two components offers only a part of the picture and process. This Toolkit (book and companion DVD), first in a series that covers our core philosophy, focuses on the component of Empowerment.

The eight key components of CCD are:

- **Relocation (Incarnational presence in the community)**
- **Reconciliation**
- **Redistribution**
- **Church-Based**
- **Listening to the Community**
- **Wholistic Approach**
- **Empowerment**
- **Leadership Development**

Often, in workshops where we teach the philosophy of CCD, people ask, "Shouldn't we be about the work of evangelizing and saving souls, instead of working with the neighborhood and all of its problems?" We would say that **CCD and empowerment *is* evangelizing.** We witness and share God's love, hope and *care in the process of addressing the wholistic needs of people and their communities.* The church sometimes preaches one thing and lives out another. We share words about God's love, while acting out racism or classism; this gives the wrong message. Some attribute this familiar quote to St. Francis: "Preach the gospel at all times, and when necessary, use words." The work of empowerment, of building relationships, and of involvement in the community, is also the work of evangelism—of saving souls.

WDJD? What did Jesus do?

Q: Why should the church be involved in the neighborhood?
Matthew 22:36-39 shares the two greatest commandments. The disciples asked Jesus, *"Teacher, which commandment in the law is the greatest?" Jesus said to them, "You shall love the Lord your God with all your heart, and with all your soul, and*

with all your mind. This is the greatest and first commandment. And a second is like it: You shall love your neighbor as yourself. On these two commandments hang all the law and the prophets." Jesus elevated the neighbor to an equal position . . . **love your neighbor as yourself,** not limited to one giver and one receiver. The disciples pushed Jesus further, asking Him, *"Who is my neighbor?"* Jesus pointed beyond the boundaries of class, race and ethnicity by offering the story of the Good Samaritan in Luke 10:25-37. There is no question that God calls us to be good neighbors—which means to get out of our safe sanctuaries and insular community framework, and be willing to reach across the boundaries of race, class, culture and economics.

Q: How can the church empower the poor? Bob Linthicum, in Building a People of Power, responds to this by saying: "It's the wrong question because no one can empower another person. The only person who can empower someone is the person him or herself. The only group that can empower a community is the community itself. **The task of the church is to join the empowerment of the community**—to participate in it, to be an integral part of it, and perhaps even to help make it happen."

Q: What is empowerment? Bob Lupton describes it this way: "Empowerment is a popular word these days. It may be a misnomer. People, like butterflies, have inbred capacity to emerge into creatures of unique beauty. But intervene in the chrysalis process while the caterpillar is undergoing the transformation and the process may be aborted. Assist the emerging butterfly as it struggles to break out of the cocoon and it may never develop the strength to fly. We may protect the cocoon from predators, even shield it from winter's hostile blast, but do more than create the conditions for timely emergence and we will cause damage. Butterflies, like people, cannot be empowered. They will emerge toward their uniquely created potential, given a conducive environment."

The World Bank describes empowerment this way: "Empowerment is the process of increasing the capacity of individuals or groups to make choices and to transform those choices into desired actions and outcomes. Central to this process are actions which both build individual and collective assets and improve the efficiency and fairness of the organizational and institutional context which governs the use of these assets."[1]

---

[1] Taken from the World Bank Empowerment website, www.worldbank.com/empowerment.

Social scientists Nanette Page and Cheryl Czuba define empowerment as a multi-dimensional social process that helps people gain control over their lives. It is a process that fosters power (that is, the capacity to implement) in people, for use in their own lives, their communities and in their society, by acting on issues that they define as important. They go on to say that empowerment occurs at the individual, group and community levels, and that empowerment itself is a process similar to a journey, one that develops as we work through it. [2]

Community developers like Kit Danley and others have struggled to unload the negative baggage of the empowerment word, and suggest using "power transfer" as a better way to describe the concept. Michael Mata calls it "mutual transformation." Rudy Carrasco notes, "We are empowered because of the power of God." Empowerment is both an individual transformation and a group transformation—it doesn't happen in isolation. Certainly, deeper conversation and work beyond this curriculum can be spent examining power and the way humans give or take it away from one another.

----

[2]Czuba, Cheryl and Page, Nanette. 1999. "Empowerment: What is It?" Journal of Extension 37 (5).

We move forward with the understanding that much more thinking and work needs to be done, and that the practice of transferring power and empowerment is ever-evolving.

Far too many of us have lived with the misconception that we can empower others, and as Lupton indicates, we have done damage. We are earthenware vessels and we make mistakes even with the best intentions. But it does not have to be this way. So we approach this curriculum on empowerment with humility, asking God to shine light on our minds and ways that we might "do no harm" (the physician's creed) to those we are called to love in our neighborhoods; but that we may be midwives of the gifts, talents, hopes and dreams God has given to each individual and community. We understand that both the process of empowerment and the process of changing how and what we do as community developers, is a journey.

Transformational community ministry is the art and discipline of recognizing, developing and calling forth the gifts, talents and resources God has already placed in the world for the benefit of all in the community. We need to measure our efforts with under-resourced communities by asking ourselves if what we are doing:

- Respects the dignity of the people involved.

- Strengthens the community in sustainable ways.

- Promotes freedom from dependency.

- Allows people to use their own resources and be self-determining.

Most of the work and exercises in this book and curriculum are focused on group action and relating to the neighborhood in groups. This is not to diminish the important work of personal empowerment and individual transformation, which happens when there is intentional commitment to developing individual relationships. Over time, these relationships can grow and become reciprocal as we acknowledge God's presence in each other and develop friendships that last despite the barriers.

In 1989, the Christian Community Development Association was formed to bring together, support, and educate Christians committed to working among the poor utilizing the Biblical philosophy of CCD. CCDA's mission is to inspire, train and connect Christians who seek to bear witness to the Kingdom of God by reclaiming and restoring under-resourced communities.

We will discover in this Toolkit, that the way we attempt to restore communities as Christians, can be harmful or helpful. The purpose of this Empowerment Toolkit is to help us move toward more effective involvement and empowerment with the poor. This requires that we look at ourselves, our under-resourced communities, and the residents of our communities through a whole new set of eyeglasses.

section two: CHURCH AND THE COMMUNITY

Note: When we use the term 'the church,' it could easily apply to a para-church, faith-based organization or related entity. In this book, we are focusing on churches within under-resourced communities. For urban-suburban relationships, we recommend Linking Arms, Linking Lives (see Books).

Tony Campolo, a well-known Christian sociologist, tells the story of visiting a church in Oakland where kids from a group called Mission Year had been working as young urban ministers. They had done a survey of the community to identify the resources in the community (such as employment centers, elder care, etc.) and went out two by two with a church member to the blocks right around the church. They introduced themselves and asked, "Are there some things we could pray together for?" The kids got some doors slammed in their faces and some No's, but also others who shared a worry about a son kicked out of school, a husband out of work, or an aunt living upstairs unable to get out because of disabilities. They prayed together, and when they left the kids noted each concern on a card. That afternoon when they assembled back at the church, they sought to make connections between the needs of people and the available resources. When Tony arrived and asked people in the neighborhood for directions to the church, they said, *"Oh, you mean that church that prays with you."*

EXERCISE: (15 minutes) In small groups, share how you think people who live in the neighborhood of your church would identify your church. How would they describe it? How would you like your church to be described? Have the groups give a brief report and if possible, note their thoughts on a large flip chart in the front of the room.

Jay von Gronigan, in <u>Communities First</u> (see Books) identifies the various ways in which churches exist in an under-resourced community: as a church *in* the community [a Fortress], a church *to* the community [a Savior], and a church *with* the community [a Partner]. Let's look at the characteristics of each:

Church "in" the community [Fortress]

- Does not desire to influence the community.
- Does not desire the community members to influence it.
- Invests efforts and resources on members.
- May be described as a "fortress" holding the outside world back; stays apart from the problems and activities of the community.
- Takes up space in the neighborhood: many members commute to services and leave again; church does not pay taxes and is a net drain on the neighborhood.

Church "to" the community [Savior]

- Desires to bless/contribute to the community on its own terms.
- Spends some (generally small) resources in the community.

- Limited access/involvement of community stakeholders in plans.
- Serves the community in ways it prefers, with outcomes it prefers, and overlooks the gifts and talents of the community.
- Takes up space in the community, performs services, does not pay taxes and generally speaking, is a neutral influence.

Church "with" the community [Partner]

- Desires to influence the community, and community stakeholders to influence the church.
- Spends significant resources (time, talent, goods) in the community.
- Uses a participatory (community and church) planning process combining desires and outcomes of both.
- Unleashes gifts, skills and resources already present in the community.
- Is a convener, partner, responder to the community.
- Net plus to community; does not pay taxes.

> EXERCISE: (in small groups) Going deeper, look at your
> church/organization and its relationship to the community.
> Which of these descriptions fits your situation? Why? Is
> there a better descriptor of your church? What do you
> desire the relationship to be? What does the leadership and
> the congregation desire the relationship to be? Report your
> findings.

How could you help more of your members or fellow congre-
gants get excited about a new way of looking at, engaging in,
and acting out God's call to love our neighbors as ourselves?
Important tools for a congregation "on the move" are:

- Studying, in small groups or together, one of the
  books in the resource list over a period of time.
- Getting a group of people to be the "prayer warriors"
  who intercede during the journey of discovery and
  mission.
- Doing some of the exercises and tools we
  "experienced" in this curriculum with your leadership
  group.
- Visiting other congregations that are actively involved
  in their communities and hearing their journey.

Different Roles for the Church *With* the Community

The church can play a variety of **roles** in relation to the community. Often the context, the giftedness and the existing relationship of the church within a particular community call for a specific kind of role. Over time, the church may play many different roles, depending on the situation. Let's examine some of them:

- **Convener** – A Convener church provides a welcoming place and space to bring people and groups together around an issue or a challenge. For example, when dealing with the violence in the community the church could be a good place to bring groups together to explore creative ways to address this issue.

- **Enabler/Facilitator** – A church serving in these roles works with community leaders and other 'voices' to identify who else should be involved; making the connections; thinking through alternative strategies.

- **Resource provider** – The assumption is usually that a resource provider church will provide money to the community. The church in this role can also provide facilities (i.e. provide use of the copy machine, etc.), and connect people to those in business and local politics, who are also important resources for a community effort. The skills and talents of the people of the church are also very important resources.

- **Partner/Advocate** – Partnering with community efforts requires special skills from the advocate church so as not to overpower community leadership, but formulate honest partnerships. This involves enabling people to attend hearings where everyone stands together as partners; attending learning conferences (like the CCDA conference) together; joining together in petitioning and visiting elected officials.

- **Participant/Recruiter** – The participant/recruiter church becomes a member of community organizations, pays dues, and recruits people for the initiatives and efforts of the community.

- **Cheerleader/Encourager** – The church in this role, is an active supporter of what the community is doing (and what it has done historically), whether the efforts were a result of the church's influence or not.

WDJD?

Mark 2:3-5 gives a great example of different roles for people and church:

Then some people came, bringing to him a paralyzed man, carried by four of them. And when they could not bring him to Jesus because of the crowd, they removed the roof above him; and after having dug through it, they let down the mat on which the paralytic lay. When Jesus saw their faith, he said to the paralytic, "Son, your sins are forgiven."

Let's take a closer look at how this passage relates to empowerment.

Analysis: Caring people are bringing a sick man to Jesus. Problems arose. It took an **idea person or instigator(s)** to have the idea to take off the roof; it took **investors** to provide the tools and the cot; it took **implementers** to do the heavy lifting; and it took **intercessors** who prayed and believed Jesus would heal the man. (This is a good outline for a sermon or talk on the subject of empowerment.)

God's Vision for Community

As we think of church and community, we must always remind ourselves of God's vision—the bold, audacious plan for people and community, shared in Isaiah 65:17-24: (The Message)

"Pay close attention now: I'm creating new heavens and a new earth. All the earlier troubles, chaos, and pain are things of the past, to be forgotten. Look ahead with joy. Anticipate what I'm creating: I'll create Jerusalem as sheer joy, create my people as pure delight. I'll take joy in Jerusalem, take delight in my people: No more sounds of weeping in the city, no cries of anguish; No more babies dying in the cradle, or old people who don't enjoy a full lifetime; One-hundredth birthdays will be considered normal—anything less will seem like a cheat. They'll build houses and move in. They'll plant fields and eat what they grow. No more building a house that some outsider takes over. No more planting fields that some enemy confiscates. For my people will be as long-lived as trees, my chosen ones will have satisfaction in their work. They won't work and have nothing come of it, they won't have children snatched out from under them. For they themselves are plantings blessed by God, with their children and grandchildren likewise God-blessed. Before they call out, I'll answer. Before they've finished speaking, I'll have heard.

EXERCISE: (Discuss) What in God's vision for our communities stands out for you? What do you think God's vision is for your community? Can you actually envision it? What is your congregation's vision? What is the community's vision? If you don't know, how could you find out what the community's vision is?

God's gift is this vision for how the community should and can be. We, as God's people, can share that hope by asking good questions in the community, eliciting that vision, starting with some first steps.

CCD's key components include **Relocation – living in solidarity with the community.** "Solidarity" implies more than residing in the same neighborhood. Presently, there is a movement among young adults who are moving into under-resourced areas and trying to reach out and minister to their poor neighbors. While their willingness to live in the under-resourced neighborhood (where they are ministering) is positive, the fact that they can leave to a better community at any time affects their ability to fully identify with their neighbors. To be truly effective we must work to not only be 'in' the neighborhood, but we must strive to be 'of' the neighborhood, which takes time to achieve.

This is important in thinking about the church, ministry, and community, because when we live in the community where we work and serve, ministry becomes an inside job. You bump into, connect and interact with neighbors on a daily basis—on the street, in the grocery store, at church. It is much easier to cross the barriers of race and class when living in solidarity with the community.

WDJD?

Acts 2:42-45 gives a good description of the early Christians and the close kind of community we should aspire to emulate: *They devoted themselves to the apostles' teaching and fellowship, to the breaking of bread and the prayers. Awe came upon everyone, because many wonders and signs were being done by the apostles. All who believed were together and had all things in common; they would sell their possessions and goods and distribute the proceeds to all, as any had need. Day by day, as they spent much time together in the temple, they broke bread at home and ate their food with glad and generous hearts, praising God and having the goodwill of all the people. And day by day the Lord added to their number those who were being saved.*

Deficiency Thinking

When members of our small, inner city church community decided that something had to be done about the lack of affordable housing in the area, they went to neighboring churches
to ask them to join in the effort. The response was, "We don't
have the resources. We don't know how. It takes too long."
These things were true for our church as well, but some of
the elders kept pushing, "We've just gotta do it!" There was a
boldness—a willingness to risk and an ability to focus, not on
the deficiencies, but on the possibilities. There was also a trust
that God would make a way out of no way.

Labels Lead to Low Outcomes

Labels like "poor people" or "poor communities" often create a one-dimensional impression of people and communities. We need to ask: What are the images, words and other labels often used to describe poor people and poor communities? And then we need to ask: What's wrong with this picture? Often, people locked in low income communities – 'labeled people' – can't see God's vision for their community, or think they have nothing to offer and begin to believe these negative labels about themselves. Some of the labeled people that come to mind are: school dropouts, the elderly, pregnant teenagers, poor people, drug abusers. Whole communities are just as easily labeled "needy," "devastated," or "blighted." What happens when people, or a community, believe these labels? How can they envision change? Seeing people and communities as "needy" has negative consequences:

- People internalize the labels they are given.
- Local relationships are destroyed as people feel they "need more professionals."
- Groups magnify the needs to gain funding.
- Needy labels create hopelessness and encourage people to feel dependent on outsiders for action.

Indeed, our 'intake forms' so often only garner the negative experiences or attributes of a person (How long they have been unemployed or whether they are school drop outs?), rather than identifying the gifts, talents, dreams and relationships that a person possesses. We need to develop new tools that enable us to gather the appropriate information that will both affirm and empower the individuals in whom we are seeking to enhance capacity. The kinds of questions we ask will greatly impact the effectiveness of our empowerment efforts.

Charity Approaches and the Arrogance of Power

Empowerment relates to power. Someone lacks a sense of power so they have to "be empowered." In the introduction, we noted that many people react negatively to the use of that word because it gives off the wrong message. We will use it here with a sense of apology and humility. Luke 1, Mary's Song, reminds us how God turned the tables upside down in terms of power dynamics: *He has brought down the powerful from their thrones and lifted up the lowly; he has filled the hungry with good things and sent the rich away empty."*

We who are in this work often have more education, more opportunity, and more resources than the people we seek to work with in low income communities. And we can often come across with an unknown arrogance. We know what needs to be done. We know the answers. We want to help people. But we get stuck in a charity/service mentality and format that does more damage than good.

EXERCISE: Have people sit in small circles. Move one chair into the middle of each circle and ask a person to stand on the chair and share a concern they have about their community or city. Take turns having different people stand on the chair in the center of the circle (be careful!). Then ask everyone else in the group to give advice on how to solve this person's concern based on their own experience. Discuss how it felt to be the people seated in the chairs, and how it felt to be the one standing on the chair getting all this advice. Reflect on/discuss how this often mirrors our well intentioned 'helping programs'.

The charity approach can give off the message that we are trying to change the poor (their lifestyle, spending patterns, etc.). This inadvertently communicates that something is wrong with them, and is in direct contradiction to the Gospel message that God indwells and loves each one of us in a unique way.

The charity approach can also create a distance between people, making it hard to have a relationship—much less a genuine friendship. Honest relationships are reciprocal ones that have built up over time; these can be empowering. Kit Danley, CCDA board member in Phoenix, Arizona, tells of such a mentoring relationship, based in love and respect, which has empowered not only the mentee, but the whole family.

This "whole-clan" approach over the years has meant that individual transformations, like the healing and change seen in Googoo's and Panda's lives, are on display before the entire family system. One teen can start making positive choices, like getting involved in I Can Do It, and convince two other cousins to join him. One aunt watches the positive growth in her sister's kids, and starts wondering how to get that in her own. Kids see their cousins having fun at The Church at the Neighbor-

hood Center, and start nagging their own moms to bring them.

"The clan starts to change because the cycle-breakers try to

bring the other family members in," Kit explains.[3]

WDJD?

In John 15:15, Jesus calls us to a different kind of relationship:

"I do not call you servants any longer, because the servant

does not know what the master is doing; but I have called you

friends, because I have made known to you everything that I

have heard from my father."

EXERCISE: Reflect/discuss whether you or your church
is doing a good job of developing real relationships/
friendships with people in the community, especially if they
are of a different race, culture, or economic status. What
does it take to develop the types of relationships Jesus calls
us to have, across racial and class divides?

---

[3]Excerpted from "The Medranos: Transforming a Clan" in Amy Sherman's The Relentless Pursuit: Stories of God's Hope, Love, and Grace in the Neighborhood.

REAL LIFE EXAMPLE: Bob Lupton tells about a Christmas experience early in his ministry: "I sat in living rooms with needy neighbors when the gift bearing families arrived, and I observed something I had never seen before. The children, of course, were all excited at the sight of the colorfully wrapped presents. The mothers were gracious to their benefactors but seemed, to me at least, to be a bit reserved. If there was a father in the home, he simply vanished. At first sight of the gift-bearers, he disappeared out the back door.

It dawned on me that something other than joyful Christmas sharing was happening here. Although the children were ecstatic, the recipient parents were struggling with a severe loss of pride. In their own homes, their impotence as providers was exposed before their children. The mothers would endure this indignity for the sake of the children, but it was often more than the fathers could take. Their failure as providers was laid bare. It was destroying what shreds of pride they were managing to hold on to. It was obvious that this charity system had to change."

EXERCISE: On a large sheet of paper, make a list of your outreach or community programs and ask these questions of each program: Does it: **Affirm** the dignity of participants? **Motivate** participants to take responsibility for their own lives? **Create** enduring hope? **Utilize** the gifts and capacities of the individuals? **Address** the underlying issues participants have or simply provide band-aid solutions? How can this exercise help you focus more on empowerment?

Invasion of the "Blessing Snatchers"

A pastor friend from Cincinnati talks about how often we well-intentioned Christians are "blessing snatchers." Jesus said, *"It is more blessed to give than to receive,"* and yet we, the ones with the resources, education and opportunities are so often the ones blessed by giving. In not enabling the people on the receiving end to share their gifts with us and the community, we deny them the blessing of sharing their gifts. We need to ask: What are the gifts that others may have to share? True partnership requires recognition of what each party has to offer.

Moving from servanthood to friendship means living out the reciprocal nature of give and take in a friendship.

Community developer and author Shane Claiborne, in Bob Lupton's book <u>Compassion, Justice and the Christian Life</u>, asks these questions: "What dilemmas do caring people encounter to faithfully carry out the teachings of Scripture and become personally involved with 'the least of these?' What are some possible alternatives to the ways we have traditionally attempted to care for the poor? How do people, programs and neighborhoods move toward reciprocal, interdependent relationships? To effect these types of changes will require new skill sets and resources, but the possibilities for good are great."

Moving from Betterment to Development

Bob Lupton defines community development as **"that which strengthens the capacity (muscle) of the neighborhood to become self-sustaining."** This also defines neighborhood empowerment. Often community development is only seen as the physical development of a community. CCD is a biblical philosophy that advocates for individual and community development that leads to empowerment.

Betterment Ministries	Development Ministries
Do for others	Enable others to do for themselves
Improve conditions	Strengthen capacity
Give a man a fish	Teach a man how to fish
Address crisis situations	Address chronic situations
Are event oriented	Are relationship oriented
Address need by giving something	Need is addressed when participant can do own problem solving
What "we do for them" focus	Focus on what participant can do for themselves (with skills, info)

Most of the programs we create to help people in need focus on making their lives 'better'. This is understandable. Often our hearts are touched when we encounter a pressing need and realize we have the capacity (yes, even the responsibility) to meet that need. We quite naturally seek ways to address that need in the most direct and immediate means at our disposal. A homeless man is hungry so we offer him food. A bright child is failing in school so we help her with her homework.

An aging widow's heat has been cut off so we pay her gas bill. These are personal acts of compassion that address an immediate, correctable need. This is where we often begin . . . with a felt need.

Transition to Betterment is not Easy

Lupton goes on to say, "It is no simple matter to convert a betterment program into a development program. It is far easier to run a free clothes closet out of a church basement than to start a retail clothing business that requires a suitable facility, professional staff, financial management systems, personnel policies and training manuals. Even if we might all agree that a thrift store is a superior means for providing affordable clothing to needy families, the money required launching it and the skill sets needed to operate it may overwhelm a compassion committee that has only a limited amount of time to volunteer. It is far easier to streamline a betterment program that serves people than to create a development system that empowers them."

Making our ministries more effective, even if we include participants in the process and look for outcomes, may still be betterment efforts and not really empowerment. Perhaps what is needed is transforming a food pantry into a food co-op, a clothes closet into a thrift store, a benevolent fund into a job bank. Or, it may be that some programs should be closed down and the people and dollar resources used more effectively in other ways.

REAL LIFE EXAMPLE: Many years ago, Bethel New Life's community board was concerned about the lack of a regular grocery store in the community and the high prices and damaged goods available at the corner quick stop. This was an issue that had come up in community meetings and conversations. The group determined to set up a food co-op that would focus on quality goods, with co-op members taking turns at gathering the goods, packaging them and manning the "store." After a year of operating it, they did an evaluation and found that they were subsidizing the operation by $25,000 a year, and that most of the users of the food co-op were not the poor, but the moderate income people who had other options (cars to get to larger grocery stores, time to participate, etc.).

They made a few adjustments which included more flexible hours for the co-op and greater discounts for lower income people. At the end of the second year, they realized that they were still not meeting their goal of providing healthy food for the low-income users of the co-op. Finally, they decided that closing the co-op and working to get a major quality grocery store to locate in their community was a more effective plan. This also freed up $25,000 to redirect into other ministry efforts.

We suggest that you take what you are learning as you go through this book and meet with a group of your ministry leaders to explore new ways of ministering to the needs of people in your community. Review the exercises and take note of new insights you have gained from this Empowerment Toolkit regarding the effectiveness of your ministry or outreach efforts. Explore ways you can work together to transition your programs from betterment activities to empowerment/ development efforts. An assessment chart for each program might look like this:

1) Assess the program as it exists now:

- What happens to a participant now?

- What do you want to have happen to a participant in the future?

- Who else should be a part of the design change (including participants)

- Are the conditions the same as they were when you began the program? Does the gap in services still exist?

- Is there any other group responding? Are we still responding to a need?

2) Define what needs to change (include participant thinking in this)

- Define success (a participant is successful when—define behavior change).

- Gather a group of stakeholders and design the program to achieve the changed behaviors you together want to see.

- Test the design ideas by running them past former program participants and getting their feedback.

3) Make the changes

- Recruit people and set the times and places to try the new program design on a small scale.

- Evaluate, modify based on the experience.

- Develop new processes and procedures.

4) Scale up

- Create a budget and raise funds.

- Add staff as needed.

- Grow through ongoing feedback and evaluation.

REAL LIFE EXAMPLE:

For many years New Prospect Missionary Baptist Church in Cincinnati operated a soup kitchen in their church basement. A group of church leaders with a desire to bridge the gap between the church and the broader community, decided to re-examine its relationship with the people it was 'serving' in the soup kitchen. "We were feeding folks, but we weren't getting to know them," explained one kitchen volunteer. "We knew nothing about their experiences, and especially about their skills and talents." So they began to initiate one-on-one conversations with the participants and were amazed at the skills of the people coming: they had carpenters, plumbers, artists, musicians, teachers, caregivers and cooks in their midst and they did not know it. Soon those with cooking skills were asked to help with the food preparation; some of the volunteers now sat at tables with others, and switched roles. Then they established a "Wall of Fame" displaying the gifts, skills and talents of people coming to the soup kitchen, which began to link people and their gifts to potential jobs in the community. Their conversations at the tables became opportunities to talk together about a vision for the community as a whole and they began to discuss ways to work together to help make that happen. The pastor commented, "We cooked and ate together, then we became friends and allies. Now we are prepared to stand together for the future of the community."

In section four, we will focus on the skills, resources and possibilities for changing our mission strategies.

Section four: EMPOWERMENT STRATEGIES (1)

It is important to *start* by looking at the people we serve and their communities with a new set of eyeglasses that enable us to see their strengths and gifts instead of their needs and deficits. Too often, if we do not begin with this mindset, we get stuck on the deficits and needs (the glass half empty), and never see the other side.

Getting New Eyeglasses – Asset Based Community Development (ABCD) ABCD originated from the pioneering work of John McKnight which sees individuals and communities as a glass half-filled with liquid.[4] In low-income

---

[4]McKnight, John L., "A Twenty-First Century Map for Healthy Communities and Families."

communities, society in general, and social programs in
particular, tend to focus on needs rather than on strengths or
capacities. We saw earlier the damaging impact this kind of
needs-based approach has on people and on communities. So
ABCD *starts* with 'half-fullness,' which are the gifts, talents and
hopes of people and the community. Learning to see people
and communities through these new eyeglasses is a great
way to approach ministry. It is consistent with the heart of the
Gospel that emphasizes God's love for each individual and
acknowledges their unique gifting and value.

Identifying the assets in individuals and the community is
called **asset mapping.** This approach unleashes new resources
and a whole new sense of abundance, providing a starting
place for empowering action.

EXERCISE: Ask people to identify what others would say are their gifts. Do this exercise in pairs, where people ask each other this question. Then list on the board some of the gifts discovered in the room. You can also do a questionnaire asking people in the group and in the community about their gifts, skills, what they want to learn, what they can teach. This exercise can also be done where people respond to, "What would your friends say are your gifts and talents?" Put each gift and talent on a 'sticky note' and post, or simply have people write them on the board. These will be valuable resources later when we begin to develop a plan to address the needs of the community. It is always amazing to see the gifts, skills and talents that exist in every group, though sometimes they have to be uncovered.

- **Gifts** – in individuals, these include gifts of the "head," the "heart," the "hands" and "relationships," which are often untapped resources in a community.

- **Associations** – these are the groups or associations (informal, focused, with volunteers) that exist in every community. Groups like bowling leagues, garden clubs, mothers groups, sports groups, etc. They are great resources you can mobilize into community action beyond their specific focus. For example, a gardening group could be asked to work with others on victory gardens (growing vegetables with a cross-generational, cross-cultural emphasis). The food grown can be shared with pantries in the community, or used to do "healthy cooking" classes. Gardeners get to do something they love, and also build relationships outside their little group.

• **Institutions, businesses, government organizations–** these are important potential partners in community empowerment. Thorough asset mapping includes identifying the leaders of these groups, talking with them, asking what their strengths are, and finding out what they want to see happen in the community. For example, community colleges are often grateful for new connections in the community. They are sometimes very willing to offer classes in a church basement if the church or community group recruits the students. Mapping out what exists in a community sometimes helps identify what is missing from a community area, such as grocery stores, banking facilities or health centers. "Food deserts," which are communities that don't have access to healthy foods stores (especially fresh fruits and vegetables), are beginning to be the focus of major community development efforts throughout our nation.

- **Physical assets** – these are parks, transportation, rivers, industrial areas, etc., which can be major opportunities for community empowerment and transformation. When seen through our new eyeglasses these potential assets can lead to leveraging significant community empowerment efforts. For example, the threatened closure of a Chicago Park District Conservatory in the community helped Bethel New Life people see what a potential asset it was. Together, Friends of the Park, the high school across the street and other community groups rallied to save it, pressing state and city officials and foundations for funding. Today, the Conservatory is a major regional draw, bringing people, business and pride into the community. A physical asset that had been ignored has now become a major resource.

- **Stories, culture, history, faith** – find times and places to share the stories of people—the community heroes and the times when people in the community came together to deal with an issue. These stories are a great gift to all, and enable people to reflect on what worked in these stories and what made these positive experiences for the community.

Getting people from different cultural groups to share their stories and their culture with each other, especially in the form of food, music, dance and style, creates a real sense of a community that shares the richness of the various cultures. Bethel New Life partnered with the Field Museum in Chicago on a project identifying the community heroes of faith, culture, justice, education, etc., and training high school kids to interview these community heroes. The interviews, along with a pair of worn shoes from each hero, became the focus of an ongoing exhibit called "Journeys from the Soul." Later, the stories became the heart of a participatory dramatic presentation presented in the community. The effort dramatically transformed the participants.

EXERCISE: Form small groups who share a neighborhood or a church in common. Take a large piece of paper and draw a map of three or four blocks with the neighborhood block or church at the center of the target area. Identify and mark the various assets found in this target area (institutions, physical assets, businesses, etc.), and again save this for future use. Identify as well, the cultural and historical assets of the community. Ask people to reflect on their insights through this exercise; save for future use.

ALTERNATE EXERCISE: Ask people in each small group to share stories of when they experienced a sense of community and then identify factors that led to that experience.

REAL LIFE EXAMPLE: Kit Danley, Neighborhood Ministries, Arizona. (Youth as Assets for Change.)

Our youth were charged with an asset mapping exercise. neighborhood was nervous about the youth because many of the ones they saw regularly were out of school or looked ominous. Armed with cameras and tape recorders they were asked to interview their own neighbors in a very distressed neighborhood. These youth were interesting and polite, some of them college students. They took about 350 photos and did 35 interviews, some lasting more than three hours. They showed a great deal of respect for their neighbors' stories and this opened up important future conversations.

When the youth created an asset map through listening, barriers were broken down. The youth were also listening for what the community desired for its future. They presented our U.S. congressman with their findings. Their project hangs on the wall in our local university, describing the efforts of local youth who listened to their community.

A special note about churches . . . Churches in the neighborhood are a tremendous asset to help bring positive change in a local community. Beyond providing buildings and facilities for meetings, the people of these congregations are their greatest resource.

In every church, there are adults, youth, and children with a variety of gifts that can be mobilized to serve the community. In addition, the church is uniquely positioned to provide leadership and inspiration that can result in community transformation. Here are just a few examples of the assets a church can provide:

a) To give **hope** – God's gift and promise is one of hope for a better future in this world and the next. Martin Luther King said, "We know finite disappointments, but we have infinite hope."

b) To invite **participation** – identifying what people want, identifying others who want the same, and linking them together.

c) To **act as a catalyst** – bringing together people who can do things together, connecting the gifts of associations, individuals, and local institutions.

d) To **prepare leaders** – equipping people who bring competency and experiences; walking along side them as they develop their gifts (see section on Leadership that Empowers).

e) To **infuse the values of the Kingdom** – instructing others that each person is loved and valued, and that God calls us all to be about the work of justice and community transformation.

f) To **cast recognition upon the community** – not themselves. Clearly in celebrating successes, "giving away the credit" is essential in dealing with politicians and others. We all glow when we are recognized or acknowledged.

g) To **be a voice or advocate for hope, peace and justice** – The church has a level of public trust; people listen to religious leaders for moral guidance on critical issues and situations.

Linking Relationships/Making Connections

Part of the next steps in discovering abundance in a community is to use what you've discovered in your asset mapping. Making linkages between individuals who share a passion for action or who share skills, and the institutions and associations you have uncovered. For example, a gifts survey may find that a number of community people love walking, but are hesitant to do it alone. So you connect these people and they begin walking together in the community. What happens when you walk? You see things, you deepen relationships, you discover some neighbors—and you get healthier

Releasing the Power of Local Associations and Organizations

As illustrated in this chart, making the connections in
a community between the church, the neighborhood
institutions, and associations needs to be a two-way street.

Note: A detailed chart and additional information can be found in: Building
Communities from the Inside Out A Path Toward Finding and Mobilizing A
Community's Assets by John P. Kretzmann and John L. McKnight, Evanston,
IL: Institute for Policy Research, (1993).

Asking the question, "What do we have to offer in exchange for what you have to offer?" is the correct approach. The sharing of resources, what we call a "win-win exchange," is less costly for the community and it's members and provides a great way to multiply impact at the same time.

REAL LIFE EXAMPLE: After some workshops on asset mapping and relating to the community, an African immigrant church in Chicago looked at its own gifts and strengths and decided that they had the gift of 'cultural pride' (as outwardly evidenced by the clothes they wore to church, their music and foods), and they also had the gift of a considerable number of men in the church..

They had a problem with the young men in the community hanging around on the street corner near their church, which was threatening to the families entering the church. They conducted interviews with businesses and other residents in the community, asking: 1) What are the two to three best things about this community? 2) What are the two to three things that need work? 3) What are you willing to help work on, and what resources do you have to share to help with the effort?

They interviewed the McDonald's across from their church, and the store employees said that they liked the mix of people in the community, but were concerned about the young men hanging around on the corner scaring away their customers. What did they have to offer? They could provide some incentives, i.e. t-shirts and McDonald's coupons, and they could host some community events. Out of this came a partnership between the church and McDonalds.

The African immigrant men made it a point to get to know the young men on the corner, and then got them involved in some projects. One week, they cleaned up a garbage-strewn vacant lot and celebrated at McDonald's afterwards. Over time, the African men taught the boys drumming, and the women taught dancing. They had a community fest on a vacant lot near the church—with food provided by McDonald's alongside their African cuisine. A sports team emerged, and McDonald's provided the t-shirts and equipment for the team. And so it goes . . . a menace and a challenge faced by this church and neighborhood business was turned into an opportunity for sharing gifts, empowerment and community building.

The Listening Conversation

Another tool of the asset based approach is called **the Listening Conversation**. Too often we in our churches decide what the community needs, and then proceed to set up a program and recruit people for it. They may come for a while, but they taper off and then we wonder why. A better approach is to find out what people in the community feel passionate about, what they want to act on, and then support that effort. The Listening Conversation chart looks like this:

Less Successful	More Successful
Start with the answer	Start with a learning conversation
Recruit people to implement the answer	Discover what people care about, how they see the situation, and what they have to offer
Use outside resources	Start with what people can offer, their gifts
Look for answers to the lack of motivation	Mobilize assets to act on the problems

A listening and learning conversation approach might have volunteers go door-to-door (preferably with a community partner) asking these questions:

1) Tell us something good that happened in the community recently.

2) What issues and concerns do you want to work on?

3) What are the gifts, capacities, and skills you have to share?

4) What are the things you'd like to learn or do?

5) What are the strong involvements you have already (associations, institutions, etc.)?

6) If you had three wishes for your community, what would they be?

7) What other contacts would you suggest (people, groups, etc.)?

EXERCISE: Discuss why this kind of listening conversation is important. What could you do with this information that would further empower the community? How would you relate this to the church? Take the asset mapping and gifts inventory from the earlier sections, identify the issues and concerns in the survey, and bring them together to tackle these issues and challenges.

REAL LIFE EXAMPLE: A CCDA member group in Waco, Texas did such a survey in their targeted community which was mixed with immigrants and the remaining white community. They discovered that a number of the white people wanted to learn Spanish, and a number of the Spanish-speaking people were willing to teach it. Because of the survey, they were able to connect the teachers with the learners. They also discovered that both sets of residents were concerned about the lack of operating streetlights in their community. This became an effort they could work together to remedy.

In summary, the ABCD approach should help us to:

- **Identify and mobilize** the assets of individuals and institutions, especially those who are "clients" of social services.
- **Build relationships** among community members and institutions, especially those that are mutually supportive.
- **Give community members more roles and power** in local institutions, resulting in citizen-led efforts.

To recap, some of the activities that enhance our journey towards empowerment include:

- **Asset Mapping** – individual gift inventories of people involved and actual physical mapping. Do it two by two. Use the information as the basis for understanding the resources available to move into action.

- **Prayer Walks** – looking around, spending time in the community, random interactions, seeing what is happening, developing relationships, and praying for and with people (remember the Mission Year kids?)

- **Listening Conversations** – these happen before starting any initiatives. Find out what people want to do, what they are passionate about, and start with that, even if it isn't high on your priority list.

- **Make Connections** – between the resources already existing in the community and the identified needs, and then link people, groups, and physical resources together to get things done. It takes much fewer outside resources to get started then you think.

Employing these methods, *in partnership with community residents and program participants,* builds a sense of community, empowers people, fosters mutual respect, and builds a more sustainable base for development.

REAL LIFE EXAMPLE: A group of 69 churches in the Twin Cities (called the Isaiah Project) began an organizing project, and conducted a week-long training program. Earlier, the organizers had connected the churches around the community issue of immigration and related concerns. The churches were asked through the organizers to address the lack of access to a Spanish- speaking church. The organizer asked the people what they could do themselves to build the church. Through the listening conversations of more than 200 visits, three themes emerged:

- People wanted to start a Spanish-speaking church in the community.
- People wanted help to address the many immigration issues affecting the community.
- People wanted to do something with economic development, such as training for small business start-ups.

Eventually the parish did open as La Comunidad Catolica del Sagrado Corazon de Jesus. The Isaiah Project also worked with the people to address the economic issues they faced as a community. They developed a Community Talent Inventory with the members of the new congregation. People named many specific community and economic skills they could contribute, including music, leadership, home visitations, supporting elders, translation, cooking, and working with children. The emerging community vision, stemming from the interviews fostered through their church, was to use a marketplace as the main strategy.

Many immigrants had business experience in their home country, but those skills were unrecognized in the social service network. Connectors approached local economic development organizations to provide training in Spanish. The multi-week program not only trained them in local business skills, but also created a community-building network of people sharing their experiences and skills.

A priest shared with them the possibility of developing businesses that would be competitive in the larger

marketplace, but that would not compete with each other.
Out of that came the plan to develop Mercado Central, a co-operatively owned building with stalls for small, individually-owned businesses—businesses built on the skills of the participants. Through creative partnerships with other local development groups and with loans they secured, a building was designed, rehabbed and occupied with stalls and small artisan stores, restaurants and specialty stalls, owned by the immigrant co-operative.

Over the years, the Mercado has grown and opened a second building. They have helped some owners relocate to larger businesses nearby, and have been an integral part of making the community an attraction for people interested in Central American culture.

Note: The full information on this inspiring story, which combines the major role of churches in community organizing and embodies the best of empowerment, can be found in: Building the Mercado Central, ABCD Institute, Acta Publications, Chicago, IL.

Section **five:** EMPOWERMENT STRATEGIES (2)

Empowerment is all about power. But it focuses on a **transfer of power;** and the concept is usually framed within the struggle for power. We in the church shy away from issues of power and transfer of power because we equate it with confrontation and friction. Think of the words that come to your mind when you mention power. They are probably words about control and domination; thinking that limits our ability to deal with the positive aspects of power.

Empowerment, as cited by social scientists, depends on two things. First, empowerment requires that power can change; second, it requires that power can expand. Understanding power as a zero-sum game that *you* get at *my* expense

cuts most of us off from power, and results in a sense of
powerlessness usually felt by the poor and disenfranchised.
Rather, we should see the *imbalance* of power, with some
having more and others less, as the problem.

This imbalance, in biblical terms, is addressed in the call
for justice when Amos cries, "Let justice roll down." As you
will see in the following section on community organizing,
a power analysis is a first step towards justice, identifying
who has the power, and how that power is used. A second
important organizing step is for poor and disenfranchised
people to realize that they have "people power" and that they
can exert it through a variety of means, including boycotts,
marches and bringing injustices to light. The experiences of
the civil rights era is an example of the snowball effect that
"people power" can produce; when small stands for justice
(like sit-ins at a lunch counter) can be the beginning of a large
movement for CHANGE.

Power in our Christian context, seeks an alternative to the
traditional struggle with power imbalance. Some seek out
dramatic examples of confronting power and injustice in an

alternative way. Others, like Paulo Freire, (Brazilian educator and writer), focus not on the power aspects, but on the strengths of people, enabling them to gain control over their own lives (and some degree of independence from the powers that be) by recognizing the skills and resources they have.

WDJD?

Jesus had to confront the issue of power and the injustice of the dominant Jewish systems of his day. His siding with the poor and oppressed put him at odds with the powers that be. But Jesus understood power in a different kind of way. Reflect on Jesus' mission statement in Luke 4: *The Spirit of the Lord is upon me because he has anointed me to bring good news to the poor. He has sent me to proclaim release to the captives and recovery of sight to the blind, to let the oppressed go free, to proclaim the year of the Lord's favor.*

How did Jesus use his power related to His mission on earth? What does it look like when we follow the example of Christ and confront issues of abuse and injustice in ways that empower those without power? Consider the following.

Community Organizing

Saul Alinsky, the father of community organizing, had several operating premises, two of which were::

- **Never do for others what they can do for themselves.**
- **There are two kinds of power: money/position and people. What poor people have are lots of people, and that's the basis of organizing.**

Much of community organizing in today's communities is done through and with churches. We start with an understanding of God's command *to let the oppressed go free.* Isaiah 58 says: *If you put an end to oppression, to every gesture of contempt, to every evil word, and give food to the hungry,* **then . . .** *"*

But for many of us and our churches, we are not connected to, or in partnership with people in the community.

REAL LIFE EXAMPLE: Kit Danley describes the journey of discernment that led their evangelical organization into rallying around the immigration issue in their community:

Possibly as a result of our Evangelical roots or our own church backgrounds, we were naïve and inexperienced in engaging the injustices that were affecting our families. Politically we were absent and not involved. In 2003 that began to change.

Proposition 200 was unveiled just two months before the November voting docket in 2003. Modeled after the controversial Proposition 187 in California, Prop. 200 would deny any public services to the undocumented and would require all Arizonians to provide state issued ID's in order to vote. Prop. 200 was unclear and purposely vague. Would this law mean our friends would have trouble getting medical care at local hospitals, or that children would be denied public education?

Caught off guard by this surge of anti-immigrant sentiment in our state, we sought to find friends in the faith community that could guide us in our response. Two things happened in 2003. Neighborhood Ministries found mentors in Valley Interfaith Project (VIP) and the local IAF and they began to teach us about community organizing. Secondly, Prop. 200 passed opening what has been a steady stream of anti-immigrant legislation and rhetoric dominating all conversation in our state legislature.

We had to learn how to describe who we were as an evangelical ministry that was committed to private expressions of faith and public advocacy on behalf of our undocumented neighbors. What did we believe and why? The legacy of our work for over 25 years has been built on the foundation of God's heart for the poor, expressed in the over 3,000 verses where God's people are called to engagement with the least, the last, and the lost of our world. The orphan, the widow and the stranger are the categories of persons we hear the Lord identifying as his most vulnerable (and most precious).

Many of our friends who have watched our work over the years in Phoenix commented, "You have no choice; this is who you are. These scriptures identify your work and your mission." As our immigrant friends, both in our ministry and in our city, continued to undergo the oppressions of a broken immigration system and the bullying of a heavy handed politic, we had to take action. This has led to a deep desire on our part to educate fellow Evangelicals, leveraging our relationships and our commitment to the community. We come in with hope for reconciliation and have found some unlikely allies.

One of the early steps in organizing is to **understand power**—who has it, what the opportunities are for a change in power, how to figure out some counter power, and understanding the people who posses power and how they use it.

REAL LIFE EXAMPLE: A bank loan to build new low-income housing in the community by Bethel New Life was denied after a long wait. A deadline was approaching. Bethel researched who was on the bank's board and what church the key bank officials attended. We contacted our bishop and suburban churches and finally found some relationships with appropriate officials. After sharing the information and the long developed plans with these church leaders, they contacted the bank and put a good word in for us. That helped, but it was our appearance at the bank when the press and the Mayor were visiting that put the pressure on the bank to reconsider their denial of our loan request. We finally got our loan commitment, but it took applying pressure (power) to make it happen.

One of the first steps in organizing is to do what is called **one-on-one's**—go out and have in-depth conversations with people. The Sojourners' Training for Change seminar emphasizes that these one-on-one conversations need to include our sharing about our own journeys to justice and action. As the Learning Conversation suggested in Section Four, Communities First espouses the following approach: Introduce yourself as a part of the church and indicate that you want to find out what they would like to see happen in the community.

Questions to ask:

> **1)** If you could wave a magic wand and make one good thing happen in the community this year, what would that be?
>
> **2)** What talents, skills, abilities, education and experiences do you have that you think could help make this happen?
>
> **3)** If other people had a similar vision, would you join with them to help make it happen?

By the time you have finished several such conversations, the possibilities for action and working together on things will become clear. After most of the interviews in the adjacent communities are completed, identify the common themes of interest, and note the gifts, talents and potential leaders. The next step is to follow up with a plan of action and a gathering to share what has been learned and discuss possible action.

When identifying good issues for justice organizing from the learning conversations, we need to uncover issues that are **concrete, winnable, immediate,** and take actions which, tackled together, will build community partnerships. Start with winnable issues and work up to the more global and challenging ones. The late Senator Paul Wellstone was a "liberal" senator who worked hard to get legislation passed, including coverage of mental illness in health care plans. His brother had suffered from mental illness, and, to his surprise, one of the most conservative senators also had a family member affected. Together they pushed in a bipartisan way for pioneering legislation in this area. He shared how to deliver results without compromising principles:

- Personalize the issues (have people share real stories of how the issue impacts them).

- Be relentless (persistent), against all odds.

- Look for unlikely allies.

- Advocate for those who do not have advocates.

REAL LIFE EXAMPLE: One thing leads to another, as shared by Bob Linthicum in Building a People of Power. When he moved to pastor a suburban Detroit church (his heart still in the city) which was adjacent to a low income community, he started out doing one-on-one interviews with his suburban parishioners. He found they cared about the elderly. So the church gathered together interested people and some elderly initiatives began to evolve.

The next year, while these efforts were continuing, some church members began having conversations and small meetings with people from the adjacent low income community in Detroit, trying to identify what they thought needed to happen. In the process, it came out that people were hungry—that welfare and unemployment checks didn't last the month long, and people needed food. People from the church and the adjoining community got together and said,

"What are we going to do about it?" After some conversation, they decided to start a soup kitchen. The meal times offered a chance for table conversations. What caused them to be hungry? Lost jobs, welfare, and end of the month shortages. Further conversations led them together to realize that hunger was not the problem, the issue was economics. They needed more jobs, more job security. What to do?

They discovered that many of the unemployed in the group had worked at the Chrysler plant that had closed several years ago. Since they had automotive repair skills, they decided to open an auto repair service. At the same time, Chrysler announced that it was ready to build a new plant in a suburban area, and they were identifying several suburban sites. That made everyone mad, because it was the plant closing in their neighborhood that had led to the unemployment problem. The group got help in researching the proposed suburban sites, as well as the existing site where the Chrysler plant had closed. They put together charts to show that the plant in the urban community would be more economical and would have greater social impact. But how would they ever get an appointment with the key officer at Chrysler?

Research uncovered that one of the church members was a close friend of the key Chrysler individual. Incredibly, the church member agreed to use his relationship to make the connection. The meeting was held, and the team presented an in-depth report, showing the benefits of the urban community site. Several weeks later, Chrysler announced that it had chosen the urban community site. Even more exciting was the officer's comments that it was the community's intervention that had been the decisive factor.

Churches can be a major part of a community of relational power that brings about significant transformation of a neighborhood and the city. Sometimes the opportunities for change happen because of a crisis, such as the closing of the only transportation line. Sometimes these opportunities come from an outside catalyst, such as an environmentally "dirty" plant moving into the community. Organizing is quicker in these instances and more focused than the long, slow work of building sustainable organizations that include efforts to gain justice and opportunity in the community.

Organizing for Justice

The Old Testament resonates with the call for justice and
freedom from oppression, and it reflects a variety of ways
to empower the "oppressed" to tackle the issues. The
collaborative process of working together on justice and
fairness issues can be not only empowering, but in the
process, the collaboration builds a strong sense of community.
It is important to identify some of these strategies for
participating in empowerment through change.

EXERCISE: Have small groups read the following passages
and identify the strategies that were used in each instance
(each group selects one passage):

Nehemiah 5:1-13   Exodus 1:8-20   Acts 15:1-29

Discuss the strategies used and report findings back to the
large group.

It's interesting to explore some of the other creative strategies
found in the Bible. Walter Wink, in <u>Jesus the Third Way</u>, reminds us of the poor man who was brought before the court
to pay his debts. He had no funds, and so was ordered to give
up his coat and outer garments. In response, he gave them

his undergarments, too, standing naked in court (which was a taboo)! He shamed them in the process and gained back his dignity. There are many such creative illustrations in our time as well.

REAL LIFE EXAMPLE: Six-hundred Nigerian village women, aged 20-90, were protesting at the gates of a large oil company near their village. They were protesting that the villages near the oil fields did not have electricity or water, and that the oil company did not hire the local young men and did not help their villages. The company responded by hiring police and security guards. In exasperation, after the company turned a deaf ear, the women contacted the press and threatened to take their clothes off in front of the oil company gates! The company reacted, and to avert the public disgrace, they agreed to hire at least 25 'village sons,' provide electricity and water in the villages, build schools and a clinic, and work with the villages to set up fish and chicken farms so that the produce could be sold in the company cafeteria. Once the company put its mind to the issue, they became creative.

Rose Marie Burger, peace activist, poet, and associate editor of Sojourners magazine, says that social justice always has an economic as well as a political component. She identifies this process for congregational or community empowerment for social justice:

1) We **listen** to the experiences of the poor; we learn that, among other things, many people work full-time but cannot afford the basics of housing, food and healthcare.

2) We **look at the context** (spiraling medical costs and inadequate minimum wage, lack of jobs and affordable housing, etc.)

3) We then **reflect** on this in light of Jesus' healing ministry and parables (i.e. workers getting good wages).

4) We **determine action**: What would Jesus do in such a situation? What actions might successfully make this situation more just?

5) Success of an **action is evaluated** based on how lives of the working poor have improved. Have actions helped restore justice and reveal the reign of God?

6) Then **identify the next issue** and start the process all over again.

Many of our congregations are unaware of the justice issues in our communities and country. Willow Creek Church in suburban Illinois took groups on "Justice Journeys," talking with people impacted by injustice, visiting places of oppression, reading books together, reflecting on the issues and actions that could be taken. Other church groups have done similar activities to raise awareness, as a first step. Still, too often we get mired in the problems and do not dig deeper to uncover the real issue. Therefore we end up with shallow responses and efforts.

WDJD?

In Exodus 31, Moses heard the cries of his people who were faced with poverty, forced labor, physical weakness, and forced to watch their children executed. If Moses had focused on any one of these problems, he would have had only partial success. Instead, he was led by God to mobilize the Israelites to address the issue behind the problem—slavery. Consider their action process to deal with slavery:

- They had a slogan: LET MY PEOPLE GO!

- They determined the objective and built a plan —
  target Pharaoh.

- They organized to carry out the plan, recruited others
  and confronted Pharaoh.

- They were assisted by external factors which put pressure on Pharaoh (God sent plagues).

- They reflected and revised the plan.

- They completed the action.

- They celebrated the success and evaluated the actions.

- They then went on to deal with the next issue.

It is very important to have short-term, intermediate outcomes
and to celebrate each minor step toward success. The work
of justice is long and slow, and interim celebrations and
acknowledgements are essential.

EXERCISE: Bring in today's or recent newspapers and look for any justice issues (or think about a recent news broadcast). You can also answer questions around problems people in the room are concerned about, like homelessness, education or health care. What are the issues behind the problems? Who are those in power; who are those not in power? Who are the winners and the losers? What are some of the actions that could be taken?

'Leader-full' Ministry – Leadership that Empowers

We can't talk about empowerment without talking about leadership. Many of us are 'leader types'— people who are listened to, who can inspire, who can sell ideas and like to get things done. Those are good qualities, but they often are person-focused and don't allow for 'leader-full' ministries and communities. The New Testament is full of admonitions to empower others to lead. 2 Timothy 2:2 says, *You have heard me teach many things that have been confirmed by many reliable witnesses. Teach these great truths to trustworthy people who are about to pass them on to others.*

Many of us are like Moses—we try to do everything ourselves. We need the Jethros (Moses' father-in-law) who can honestly help us examine what we are doing.

EXERCISE: In small groups, read Exodus 18:13-27 and discuss. What was wrong with how Moses was doing things? What did Jethro suggest that Moses do differently? Are there instances in our own situations when we are leading like Moses? How/what can we change?

Sometimes our willingness to empower others may be undermined by our fear that it might diminish our own power or status, but by empowering others, we are freed to do even more. **Multiplication of leadership via leadership development** is the key to greater community impact. But it takes courage to listen to advice like Moses listened to Jethro, which resulted in more effective, empowering leadership.

Ephesians 4:11-13 tells us we also need the various gifts and talents of many other people to make things happen. *He is the one who gave these gifts to the church: the apostles, the prophets, the evangelists, and the pastors and teachers. Their responsibility is to equip God's people to do his work and build up the church, the body of Christ, until we come to such unity in our faith and knowledge of God's Son that we will be mature and full grown in the Lord, measuring up to the full stature of Christ.*

What is clear to those of us who have been in this field a long time, is that leadership development has to be an *intentional* part of what we do. It takes time, resources and effort, to continuously develop new leaders—especially the next generation of young leaders. We must expose them to other groups and places, i.e. bring our developing leaders to the CCDA National Conference and National Student Leadership Intensive. It requires giving new and young leaders opportunities to make decisions and come to different conclusions than we would. Many community organizing efforts rotate leadership over short periods of time, sharing the opportunity to lead meetings with others. This important process has been broken down as follows:

- **Identify** potential leaders, or existing emerging leaders (not everyone is going to be a leader).

- **Equip** potential leaders with experiences, some of your time, and opportunities.

- **Mobilize** emerging leaders to step to the plate and begin taking on roles.

- **Support** and encourage new leaders as they move into leadership roles.

REAL LIFE EXAMPLE:#1: CCDA Board member Rudy Carrasco shared about his youth leadership development and empowerment ministry:

At Harambee we have various young people, staff members and board members who are good examples of empowered individuals. I like to showcase those who have taken the capacity-building we have offered them and translated that into measurable accomplishments. One of the ways we do this is to engage the youth in fundraising. There are often very measurable success stories as the youth demonstrate their ownership of the work by utilizing the knowledge and skills they have gained to bring in donations through creative fundraising activities.

REAL LIFE EXAMPLE:#2: Bethel New Life sponsored community leadership training sessions with a Chicago group, called Citizen Leaders. Bethel identified people in the community who were leading block clubs, school groups or groups in their churches, and asked if they were interested in getting more training to enhance their natural leadership skills. They were also asked to gather a number of people they were working with in their own group. One week these leaders would attend training workshops, the next week they would train their group with what they had learned. The training presented over a series of sessions included: identifying issues and challenges, options for dealing with challenges, encouraging other leaders, running effective meetings, identifying resources and other valuable information.

The group itself became peer leaders with each other as they shared their progress. In the last sessions they learned to write a brief proposal for a project their home group wanted to do. With some coaching to clarify the projects, each leader was given $500 for the project. At graduation several months later, they reported on the progress of their project.

Out of this main effort came a number of mini-community projects:

- One woman's group took a garbage-strewn vacant lot on their block (which they acquired from the city for one dollar!) and transformed it into a garden and gathering space with a gazebo which they built using the funds they were given. Many years later it is still a gathering place for that block and a beautiful garden. The leader now owns a small coffee shop in the community which is also another gathering place.

- Another woman took her challenging experience of becoming a certified foster care provider and turned that into a not-for-profit organization, assisting others in becoming foster care providers and training them.

- A school leader, worried about the young men hanging around outside the elementary school, trained the youth to become crossing guards and security officers, and used the funds to buy impressive jackets for the trained young men to wear as symbols of their status. Some got jobs related to security out of that experience.

These examples remind us to always include leadership development in our plans for empowerment. CCDA uses the following poem to serve as a perfect reminder of what Christian Community Development is all about—the kind of leadership that transforms lives and communities.:

Go to the people,
Live among them,
Learn from them,
Love them,
Start with what they know,
Build on what they have:
But of the best leaders,
When their task is done,
The people will remark
"We have done it ourselves."

EXERCISE: In small groups or sharing as a large group, discuss: What initially stands out for you in this poem? What additional thoughts and insights do you learn about empowerment from this poem? How does this embody the kind of empowerment and leadership we have been talking about in this workbook?

addendum

Nehemiah

The book Nehemiah offers a great extended study for your group, especially the first six chapters, in terms of leadership, mobilizing indigenous people for action, and empowerment. Robert Lupton's Renewing the City and Robert Linthicum's Building a People of Power are rich studies on the book of Nehemiah. The following summary (taken from another of Linthicum's books, Transforming Power) outlines the process of empowerment that Nehemiah employed with the people.

Iron rule of organizing: Never do for others what they can do for themselves. (Neh. 1-6)

- Began by building relationships—Nehemiah heard a lot of bad news, but he simply kept asking questions, probing and listening to the stories people had to tell.

- Internalized the pain—sat down and wept.

- Prayed for the people—fasted and prayed.

- Considered the resources—was cupbearer of the King.

- Built first actions on relationships—started with what he had and identified influential leaders.

- Assessed the situation personally—engaged in personal interaction.

- Publicly articulated the problem (arising out of what was heard from the people).

- Turned the problem into an issue—said, "Come, and let us rebuild the wall of Jerusalem, so that we no longer suffer disgrace."

- People determined the issue and committed to the common good. They said, "Let us start rebuilding . .

- People created their own strategy—involved each family and used self interest.

- People carried out the action—they were stakeholders.

- People confronted and defeated systems—the threat of violence and political opposition.

- Nehemiah confronted the principalities and powers of Israel—short term loans; foreclosure; stories of exploitation; covenant..

- The people celebrated their victory.

Creating a Community Agenda for Change:
Special Exercise

1) Gather people from your
   church and neighborhood.

When the park is clean

When kids have places to play

2) On a large piece of paper,
   draw a circle that everyone
   can see. Call the circle a Victory
   Circle. Ask the participants
   to complete this statement: Life in this community will be
   better when _____.
   List their ideas in different colors on the circle.

3) From the list, choose a few victories that this group can
   achieve fairly quickly (within six months).

4) Take another sheet and draw a second circle. Divide the
   circle into quarters. Label the top left quarter **strengths**,
   and the lower left **weaknesses**. The left half represents the
   condition of the group. List your groups' strengths and
   weaknesses to accomplish what is in the circle.

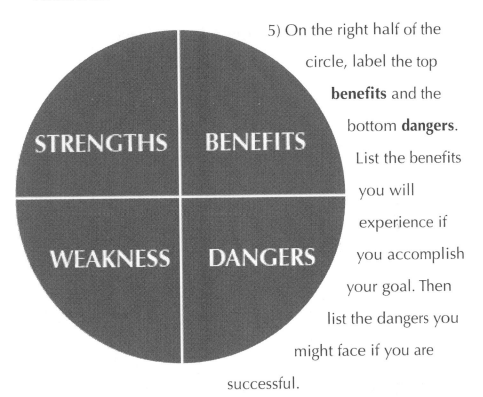

5) On the right half of the circle, label the top **benefits** and the bottom **dangers**. List the benefits you will experience if you accomplish your goal. Then list the dangers you might face if you are successful.

6) Take another sheet and draw a circle. Call the circle **commitments**. Based on the Victory circle, list a few things the group is committed to accomplishing.

a) Cluster these commitments into three groups that make sense to participants. Which items belong together?

b) Invite people to self select into the three different groups based on the tasks that interest them most.

c) Have each group begin to **work out action steps** to accomplish the things on their lists and then **create a schedule** for continuing the actions steps over the next six months.

d) Bring the groups back together and **integrate their results into one big calendar** that includes planning for all three groups. This will give an opportunity to see where the groups can coordinate or where you need to add more action steps. Have someone **create a master calendar and scorecard** to monitor progress of all teams.

e) Bring the groups back **on a monthly basis** to review progress. At the end of six months, have the group **repeat the process.**

*reprinted from <u>Communities First</u> materials

Time Banking – Building community through sharing (skills, gifts, needs, and wants)

.

Time banking, now an international movement started by Dr. Edgar Kahn, is based on the principle of giving and receiving in a community, where giving and receiving are mutually balancing actions. It started with the simple notion of connecting people who have gifts of time, skills, and energy to share, but want to barter these gifts for items and activities they need and want. For example, a senior has time and patience to baby sit, or cook or mend clothes, but needs help to get her lawn mowed or a ride to a doctor's appointment. It is the old bartering system, but by setting up a mechanism (the Time Bank) to identify the hours worked (deposited in the Time Bank) choices are now available that provide ways to use the "savings". Time banking is now practiced in communities all over the world.

Time banking can be set up very informally at first to build a caring and sharing community context, or it can be more "planfully" organized with assistance from TimeBank.org's materials and suggestions.

The five core values of Time Banking are very similar to the values of our Christian faith, and utilize the understanding of asset based community development. They are:

1) **Assets**—We are all assets and we all have something to give.

2) **Redefining work**—Some work is beyond price. Work has to be redefined to value whatever it takes to raise healthy children, build strong families, revitalize neighborhoods, make democracy work, advance social justice, and make the planet sustainable. That kind of work needs to be honored, recorded and rewarded.

3) **Reciprocity**—Helping works better as a two-way street. Change the question "How can I help you?" to "How can we help each other build the kind of world we both want to live in?"

4) **Social Networks**—We need to build networks that possess deep roots of trust and commitment; people with these types of special relationships help each other transform communities.

5) **Respect**—Every human being matters. Respect underlies freedom of speech, freedom of religion, and everything we value. Respect supplies the heart and soul of democracy. When respect is denied to anyone, we all are injured. We must respect where people are in the moment, not where we hope they will be at some future point.

BOOKS

Asset Based Strategies for Faith Communities. Susan Rans and Hilary Altman. Acta Publications, Chicago. actapublications@aol.com.

Building Communities from the Inside Out: A Path Toward Finding and Mobilizing a Community's Assets. John P. Kretzmann and John L. McKnight. Acta Press, Chicago, 1993.

Building a People of Power: Equipping Churches to Transform their Communities. Robert Linthicum. Authentic, World Vision. 2005.

Building the Mercado Central: A Community Building Workbook, Geralyn Sheehan. Acta Press, Chicago, 2003.

Communities First. Edited by Jay Van Groningen. Christian Reformed World Relief Committee, CRWRC, Michigan.

Compassion, Justice and the Christian Life. Robert Lupton. Regal Press, 2007.

Linking Arms, Linking Lives. Ron Sider, John Perkins, Wayne Gordon, F. Albert Tizon. Baker Books, 2008.

Renewing the City. Robert D Lupton. Inter-Varsity Press, 2005.

The Power of Asset Mapping: How Your Congregation Can Act on its Gifts. Luther Snow. The Alban Institute, 2004.

The Relentless Pursuit: Stories of God's Hope, Love, and Grace in the Neighborhood. Amy L. Sherman. Dawson Media, 2007.

Made in the USA
San Bernardino, CA
10 August 2015